IDEAS AND INVENTIONS

FOOD AND FARMING

Feeding an Expanding World

Philip Wilkinson
Illustrated by Robert Ingpen

Chrysalis Children's Books

First published in the UK in 2005 by
Chrysalis Children's Books
An imprint of Chrysalis Books Group Plc,
The Chrysalis Building, Bramley Road, London W10 6SP

ISBN   1 84458 211 6

British Library Cataloguing in Publication Data
for this book is available from the British Library.

Editorial Manager: Joyce Bentley
Senior Editor: Rasha Elsaeed
Series Editor: Jon Richards
Editorial Assistant: Camilla Lloyd
Designed by: Tall Tree Ltd
Cover Make-up: Wladek Szechter

Previously published in four volumes for Dragon's World *Caves to Cathedrals,
Science & Power, Scrolls to Computers, Wheels to Rockets*

Printed in China

10 9 8 7 6 5 4 3 2 1

CONTENTS

Introduction

When you feel hungry you know just what to do. Most families have cupboards full of food in the kitchen. You can be eating a snack in seconds or cooking a meal in minutes. Our earliest ancestors did not have it as easy as this. If they wanted food they had to go out to find it – literally, because the first humans fed their families by hunting wild animals and gathering plants.

Hunting and gathering was hard. The search for food took up a lot of people's lives and much of their energy. Yet the hunter-gatherers survived. People got to know which plants were good to eat, and where the best food grew. They learned the habits of animals and were able to hunt powerful creatures, like wild oxen, without getting hurt themselves. They also developed a range of stone tools to help them prepare their food.

Gradually, however, groups of people decided that they wanted more control over their supply of food. They realized that they could achieve this by growing crops – in other words, they became the world's first farmers. This was a huge turning point in the history of the human race. It meant

that people could settle down in one place rather than wander around hunting and gathering. Farming led to the appearance of the first towns and villages.

Ever since people began to cultivate crops 12,000 years ago, farmers have been improving their methods so that they can produce food more easily. This has meant developing new tools, such as the plough, getting the best out of the soil by growing crops in a special order or rotation and selecting different animals to use and raise, from sheep and goats to pigs and cattle.

Some of the biggest advances came around 200 years ago, when the population rose quickly in western Europe. Inventors developed machines, such as reapers, so that farmers could work more quickly. The farmers themselves experimented with new ways of growing crops and new breeds of livestock. The result was the more scientific, more efficient kind of agriculture that enables quite a small workforce to produce food in vast quantities – the kind of farming that still supplies the tables of much of the planet and keeps our fridges and kitchen cupboards stocked today.

PHILIP WILKINSON

THE FIRST TOOLS

Millions of years ago, our ancestors began to walk on two legs and to use stones as weapons and tools. From that time, human history has been firmly bound up with the discovery and invention of new tools.

When the dinosaurs died out 65 million years ago, primitive mammals began to take over the Earth. Some species did not survive and eventually became extinct. Others evolved into the mammals on the Earth today. One group of mammals developed in quite a different way from the others to become the early

△ *Flint spearheads were efficient tools for killing large animals.*

◁ *Sharp bone, flint and wood could be used for cutting and skinning animals.*

ancestors of humanity. About 60 million years ago, this group of squirrel-like creatures took to the trees. They developed strong limbs to climb and swing in the branches. Their front paws became flexible so that they could grasp fruit and insects. Life up in the trees was dangerous because the leaves could hide enemies. The brains of these tree-dwellers began to expand so that they could out-think predators.

Some of these mammals moved down from the trees to live on the ground about 15 million years ago. Perhaps food in the forests had grown scarce and these

HOW THE FIRST PEOPLE DEVELOPED

2,000,000 years ago
Homo habilis appeared in Africa. He was the first hominid to make tools.

1,500,000 to 500,000 years ago
Homo erectus spread through Africa, Asia and Europe. He was the first hominid to use fire, live in caves and build huts.

400,000 to 50,000 years ago
Homo sapiens lived in Africa, Asia and Europe.

100,000 to 30,000 years ago
Homo sapiens Neanderthalis, a species of *Homo sapiens*, appeared.

From 50,000 years ago
Homo sapiens sapiens first appeared in Africa, then spread to Europe about 35,000 years ago. This hominid was the direct ancestor of modern people.

creatures had to come down from the trees to feed. By now, they looked more like apes. By four million years ago, these mammals, known as 'hominids', had begun to walk on two legs. Their front paws had developed into hands with fingers capable of holding sticks and stones. All the inventions and discoveries that we know and take for granted today stemmed from these simple beginnings.

FINDING TOOLS

The hominid's upright posture was a very important development. Now their hands were free to make and use tools. Like many early discoveries, the use of tools probably began by accident. Perhaps the hominids realized that sticks were useful for digging up roots. Stones could be used to crush or chop. Before long, someone noticed that some stones had sharp edges which could be used to cut up meats and plants.

At first, the hominids found suitable sticks and stones when they needed them. Someone who wanted to cut up a piece of meat found a sharp-edged stone which happened to be lying around. When the meat was cut, the stone was discarded.

MAKING TOOLS

The next stage required more thought. The early hominids realized that they did not have to look for sharp stones. They could use one stone to chip away at another until it had a sharp edge. Early tool-making had begun. This was an important moment – for the first time, a group of mammals did not have to rely on their own teeth and claws to kill and cut up food. They could use tools to help them perform more efficiently.

As far as we know, the first tool-makers lived in East Africa about two million years ago. Flint tools have been found on the shores of Lake Turkana in northern Kenya and in the Olduvai Gorge near Lake Victoria. The hominid species that made these early tools has been named *Homo habilis*, which means 'handy' or 'tool-making' man. *Homo habilis* could stand and walk upright and his brain was nearly half the size of the modern human brain. These hominids were the first true human ancestors.

The tools of these early people were simple pebbles with flakes chipped away to form a cutting edge. Some tools had long, flat blades. Others had shorter, more pointed ends. Early people did not

▷ *Early people made a variety of tools but the hand-axe was the most common type. It had two sharp edges and could be used for cutting, grinding, scraping and pounding.*

Pebble tools
*Small tools made by removing
a few chips from a pebble.*

Blade tools
*Flakes of flint worked
to make tools for
cutting and boring.*

Core tools
*Tools made by removing flakes
from a core of flint.*

Flake tools
*Small cutters and scrapers made
from flakes cut from a flint core.*

grow or farm any food, so they had to find food for every meal and most of their time was spent hunting small mammals and grubbing around to find plants. Tools would have been useful for killing and skinning animals, cutting up meat and shredding plants. People also needed shelter and clothing to keep them warm. Sharp tools would help them cut branches to make shelters. Flat-bladed tools would have been useful for scraping animal skins to make simple clothes.

the off-cuts are called 'flake-tools'. Once people realized that they could shape flint in different ways they could make special tools for each job.

HAND-AXES

The development from the earliest pebble tools to specialized tools took thousands of years. The first more elaborate tool was an oval hand tool with a double-sided edge. This led to the development of the 'hand-axe'. Hand-axes were made

Many types of stone were used to make tools, but flint was the best because it gave a tough, hard edge. People had to search for pieces of flint the right size and shape to make the tools they wanted.

CHOPPERS, CUTTERS AND SCRAPERS

At first, people made general-purpose tools which could be used for chopping, cutting and scraping. The size and shape of the tool depended on the stone it was cut from. Then, people discovered that they could get more than one tool from a single stone.

Many early tools were made from flint, a hard stone which breaks up into fragments with sharp edges. To make tools, people chipped flakes off the flint. Some flakes were long and sharp enough to make into separate tools. The shaped piece of flint is known as a 'core tool'. Tools made from

by chipping away small flakes from a stone, usually with a piece of bone or hard wood. The hand-axe was oval or triangular. One end was chipped away to a fine point. The other end was broad enough to be gripped in the hand.

The first hand-axes were probably made in Africa between 1.4 and 1.2 million years ago. By this time, a new species of human had replaced *Homo habilis*. This species is known as *Homo erectus*, or 'upright man'. These people lived between 1.5 million and 500,000 years ago and spread from Africa into Asia and Europe, where examples of hand-axes have been found. People living in the Far East do not seem to have discovered hand-axes, however. Remains found at a *Homo erectus* site at the Choukoutien cave, near Bejing in China, shows that the people there had only simple chopping tools.

THE RIGHT TOOL FOR THE JOB

Tools could be shaped more precisely with bone or wood than they could by simply banging them with another stone.

Flakes from core tools could be shaped into very sharp, thin knives. People learned to chip the core carefully so that the flakes were the shape they wanted. For example, if the core was shaped into a curved oval, a long strip could be cut from the curved side. The flake would be rounded with thin sharp edges. It could be used as a knife or a scraping tool without any further shaping.

This is called the 'Levalloisian' method of tool-making, after a site near Paris

STONE-WORKING TECHNIQUES

Early people used several methods of making stone tools. Some tools were made by simply banging one stone against another. For others, tiny flakes were chipped off to give a very sharp edge. As tool-making progressed, people learned to use a variety of methods to produce the effect they wanted.

A pebble was used to remove flakes from another stone.

Wooden hammers were sometimes used to get a more precise shape.

To get a razor-sharp edge, tiny flakes were removed using a bone 'burin' with a sharp point.

Levalloisian technique
When the right stone had been found (1), the core was shaped very precisely (2-5). The arrows show the direction of the strokes. The tool-maker aimed a single blow with a stone to remove a finished sharp tool (6).

1

2

3

4

5

6

where examples of these tools were found. Now people could make different tools to suit their needs. Hand-axes were heavier than flake tools and could be used as weapons against enemies as well as for hunting and chopping wood. Light, sharp flake tools were better for cutting, skinning, slicing and shredding.

NEANDERTHAL TOOLS

Neanderthal people appeared about 100,000 years ago. They are named after

the Neander Valley in Germany, where their bones were first found. They were a sub-species of *Homo sapiens*, or 'wise man', the species from which modern human beings are descended. Neanderthal

▷ *Hunters combined flint with other materials to make weapons. From left to right:*
1 Serrated flint knife
2 Axe with a stone head and a shaft made of antler
3 Bone weapon
4 & 5 Bone harpoons attached to shafts with twine
6 Finely carved flint knife

OLDUVAI GORGE

Much of what we know about the first hominids comes from studies made at Olduvai Gorge in northern Tanzania. Millions of years ago, there was a large lake here. Animals living in the area, including the early hominids, came to the lake to drink. Rivers flowing into the lake deposited silt. These silt deposits gradually filled the lake up and rock layers began to form. All this took millions of years to happen. Then a river began to cut its way through the rock, gradually forming what is now the Olduvai Gorge. As the gorge deepened, more and more ancient rock layers were exposed. They contain the fossilized remains of animals that lived in the area in the past.

Studies were made of the fossils but at first no one realized that there were hominid remains among them. Louis (1903–71) and Mary (1913–96) Leakey were fossil experts or 'palaeontologists' studying the gorge in the 1930s. They found fragments of fossilized bone which proved to be from early hominids. The Leakeys named their find *Homo habilis*. In 1972, the Leakeys' son, Richard (1944–), found the skull and leg bones of a two-million-year-old *Homo habilis*. Examples of *Homo erectus* were found in higher layers of rock, showing that they were more recent. Many different types of tools were found in the gorge. Their position in the rock layers helped to date them and show which hominids made them.

2   3   4   5   6

TOOLS FOR BORING

The discovery of metal allowed tool-makers to make stronger tools with a narrower point.

A metal awl with a wooden handle could pierce the toughest materials without breaking (1-3).

A more efficient way of making a hole was to use a bow drill (4). The drill was pushed down hard. As the twine untwisted, the drill turned, forcing the bit into the material.

To be more effective, the tool had to remove some of the material from the hole. The ancient Assyrians and the Romans both used drills with two-edged bits or with spoon bits (5) which did this.

people looked brutish, but they had bigger brains than modern people and were quite intelligent. They spread throughout western Asia and Europe. At this time, the world was in the grip of an Ice Age. Neanderthal people probably wore animal skins to keep warm. Flint scrapers have been found at their sites. These could have been used for scraping fat from skins to make them into clothing.

◁ *Tools and weapons*
1 *Antler axe*
2 *Stone blade*
3 *Serrated stone saw*
4 *Bone awl*
5 *Flint arrowheads*
6 *Bone harpoon head*
7 *Flint hand-axe*
8 *Bone barbed fish hook*
9 *Stone adze with wooden handle*

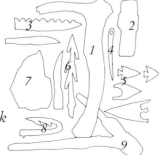

The Neanderthals were the first to make proper use of flake tools. In fact, they cut the flakes they wanted and then threw away the core. They did not just pick up pieces of flint at random, but searched until they found stones suitable for cutting off flakes exactly the right shape and size for the purpose. From these flakes, they made small spear-heads, hand-axes and knives. Their knives had one sharp edge and one blunt edge, like modern knives. The Neanderthals also developed a type of saw by cutting notches in the sharp edge of a flint blade.

HUMAN ANCESTORS

A new species of people appeared about 50,000 years ago. These people, called *Homo sapiens sapiens*, are our own direct ancestors. They began to produce a variety of tools and weapons. Some of these tools and weapons were made from bone instead of stone. They also designed a range of implements for making their tools. They used knives, bone or wooden hammers, and a bone tool called a 'burin', which was used for cutting tiny flakes to get a very sharp finish.

These implements allowed people to make far more delicate and precisely shaped tools than before. They still made knives and other tools from flint, but they could also shape pieces of bone into pins, needles, burins and awls. They could now make clothes by sewing skins together. Tool-makers also learned how to join a blade or axe head to a wooden shaft. They used this technique, known as 'hafting', to make arrows, spears and axes.

THE FIRST FARMERS

About 12,000 years ago, groups of hunters had spread to most parts of the world. Then, 2,000 years later, there was a major new development in world history. Instead of moving from place to place following herds of animals, people began to settle down and farm the land. These first farmers needed a whole new range of tools for preparing the land and harvesting crops. They made axes for clearing forests, hoes to turn the soil, and sickles for cutting the crops.

The sickle had a long, crescent-shaped blade and a wooden handle. It was one of the most important tools for these early farmers but it was often difficult to find long pieces of flint to make the blade. The ancient Egyptians got around this problem by making wooden sickles with a row of flint blades along the cutting edge.

The early farmers needed a plentiful supply of flint to make their tools. Until this time, people had relied on searching for suitable flints on the ground. Now,

THE DEVELOPMENT OF THE SICKLE

The first sickles were probably made about 10,000 years ago in Mesopotamia.

The ancient Egyptians used a wooden shaft with a row of flint blades to form the cutting edge.

△ *Copper-bladed sickles were not very strong and were difficult to keep sharp. People started working copper about 8,000 years ago.*

Sickles made of bronze (a much harder metal) were used by the Egyptians and Babylonians from about 3400 BC onwards.

This iron sickle, dating from about 3,000 years ago, is very similar to the shape of those used for harvesting in Europe until well into the nineteenth century.

CLOTHES

Homo sapiens sapiens used their more sophisticated tools to make clothes from animal skins. First, the skins had to be prepared so that they did not crack and fall apart. The skin was stretched out on the ground and scraped clean of fat with a scraper tool. Then, it was smoothed with a bone tool to make it more supple.

When the skin was ready to use, it was cut to shape with stone knives. Holes were punched along the edges with an awl. The edges of the skins were sewn together using a bone needle and a length of sinew.

The skins were used to make tunics or coats, and skirts or trousers.

The edges of the garments were sometimes decorated with shells and people wore necklaces made from shells or bone.

they began to mine underground. Miners sunk shafts about nine metres deep into the earth and dug out the best flint with picks made from deer antlers.

METAL TOOLS

Then, about 8,000 years ago, a new and exciting advance was made in western Asia. This was the discovery of metal and its uses, and it opened up a whole new range of possibilities.

Copper was the first metal to be used in most early civilizations. It was a soft metal which was easy to shape but not very strong. Early metal workers discovered that hammering the cold metal made it stronger. Copper mixed with other metals, such as nickel or tin, was stronger than copper on its own. Bronze was the first 'alloy', or mixture of more than one metal. Iron later replaced other metals for many tools and weapons.

Some metal tools were copies of older stone or wooden tools – copper and bronze crescent-shaped sickles began to replace wooden ones. Other metal tools were completely new designs.

WORKING IN WOOD

As civilization progressed, people found that they needed more things to make life comfortable. They wanted to trade, so they needed ships. They built permanent houses instead of rough shelters. They needed a large range of household objects. Many of these things were made from wood. Carpenters were among the most important craft-workers of ancient times and they needed a range of tools.

Many early tools have been lost, but archaeologists have found important evidence at an ancient Assyrian site. For cutting and shaping wood, Assyrian carpenters used metal axes, saws, chisels and the 'adze', a tool with an arched blade at right-angles to the handle.

The craft-workers of ancient Greece must have had a variety of tools for the skilled work they did. Paintings on Greek pottery show carpenters, cobblers and metal-workers, together with the tools they used. Sculptors needed tools to shape the magnificent statues and carvings we can still see today. They must have had fairly sophisticated tools to achieve this range of work. It is hard to be sure what these tools were like because little evidence has emerged from Greece itself.

SPREADING IDEAS

Most of our knowledge about tools in the ancient world comes from the Romans. The Romans adopted many Greek ideas when they conquered the Greek empire, so it is likely that many of their tools are based on Greek ones. Roman carpenters had frame-saws and bow-saws for cutting wood, and two types of drill. The plane was used for the first time in the Roman period. They also had hammers, chisels, axes, adzes and rasps.

By the Middle Ages, tools had progressed still further. Carpenters began to use a vice for holding wood while they worked on it, and a lathe for turning wood while they shaped it. They also used a brace for holding and turning a drill bit, and a T-shaped augur for boring wide holes. Standard tools became more varied. There were different types of saws, hammers, axes, adzes, chisels and rasps for doing different jobs. Many of the tools were similar to those found in the carpenter's workshop today. Hand tools had come a long way since the first crudely carved pebble.

▷ *This medieval carpenter is turning a piece of wood on a lathe driven by a bow. This works on the same principle as the bow drill. Nearly everything was made of wood in medieval times, so the carpenter needed a wide range of tools.*

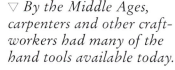

▽ *By the Middle Ages, carpenters and other craft-workers had many of the hand tools available today.*

1 Augur
2 Brace and bit
3 Froe for splitting wood
4 Clamp
5 Fretsaw
6 Rasp
7 Plane
8 Bow drill
9 Axe

6

7

19

8

9

GROWING FOOD

*Gradually, people discovered that they
could produce their own food instead of
wandering in search of it.
As they settled down together in one place,
communities began to develop.*

People lived by hunting or gathering food for nearly two million years. They discovered which plants were edible and learned to follow herds of migrating animals over long distances. But eventually most groups of people stopped this nomadic way of life and became farmers.

When the early hominids appeared, the world was in the grip of the last Ice Age. Foods such as leaves, fruit, roots, berries and nuts were plentiful in warmer areas but as people spread north into icy regions, they found that they could only gather plants for a short part of the year. For the rest of the time, they had to rely on hunting wild animals, such as the mammoth and the reindeer which could survive in these conditions. These animals also had to find food in a hostile climate and they were constantly on the move.

△ *Goats were among the first animals to be domesticated to provide meat, milk and skins.*

▷ *Early farmers cleared land by hacking down trees and shrubs, and burning the undergrowth. 'Slash and burn agriculture', as this is known, is still practised today in some parts of the world.*

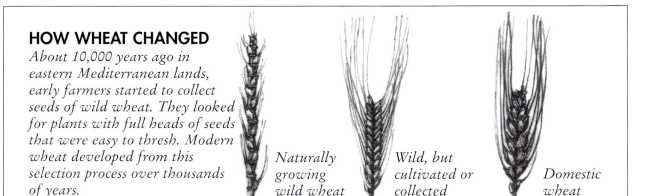

HOW WHEAT CHANGED

About 10,000 years ago in eastern Mediterranean lands, early farmers started to collect seeds of wild wheat. They looked for plants with full heads of seeds that were easy to thresh. Modern wheat developed from this selection process over thousands of years.

Naturally growing wild wheat

Wild, but cultivated or collected

Domestic wheat

Then, about 15,000 years ago, the climate began to change. The weather gradually became warmer and the ice began to melt. First, coniferous forests began to spread northwards. Then, as the weather became warmer still, forests of deciduous trees such as oaks began to grow and flourish. Ice Age animals died out or moved north, and new animals such as deer, elk and wild pig appeared in the forests. Glaciers melted, leaving lakes where fish and waterfowl could live.

A NEW SOURCE OF FOOD

Life became more comfortable, but it also presented new problems. There was less meat because the animals living in the forests were much smaller and harder to track. People had to look for other sources of food. Some groups discovered that if they lived on the banks of a lake or a river, they could take advantage of the water and the land. They learned to fish and catch waterfowl. They made dug-out canoes and a new range of tools such as harpoons and fish hooks. In other places, hunters studied the movements of forest creatures and learned to track them. These animals did not migrate over long distances so there was now no need for people to follow herds. People began to settle in more permanent groups.

At about the same time, people started

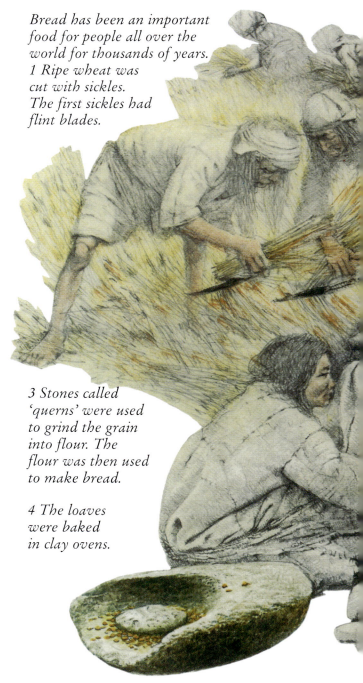

Bread has been an important food for people all over the world for thousands of years.
1 Ripe wheat was cut with sickles. The first sickles had flint blades.

3 Stones called 'querns' were used to grind the grain into flour. The flour was then used to make bread.

4 The loaves were baked in clay ovens.

to realize that they could provide their own food. They could sow seeds and harvest a crop. They could domesticate animals so there was always a supply of meat without having to hunt.

2 The grain was separated from the stalks and outer husk, or 'chaff', by tossing the wheat in the air. The lighter chaff blew away, leaving the grain behind.

WHERE DID FARMING START?

Farming probably started in several places at the same time. We know that there were farming communities in eastern Mediterranean lands by about 10,000 BC. Early forms of wheat and barley grew wild on hillsides. These wild grasses had large seeds which could be ground to make flour. People noticed that

seeds accidentally dropped near their camps began to grow. The soil around the camp had been disturbed and this helped their growth. They began to prepare plots of land by removing other plants and turning the soil over. They sowed seeds from the wild grasses. Soon they had flourishing fields of cereal crops. Crops were cut with a sickle or a bone reaping knife – its blade had flint teeth along it.

farmers became so efficient that they could grow more wheat than they needed to feed themselves and their families. This was an important development. For the first time, some people could turn their attention to other types of work. Craft-workers began to make pottery, tools, baskets and jewellery, and to work in wood. They traded with the farmers, exchanging these goods for food.

△ *Domesticated herds must be protected from wild animals and led to water and grazing every day.*

IMPROVING ON NATURE

Early farmers began to improve on the wild grasses. The seeds of wild wheat scatter very easily as soon as they are ripe. This is nature's way of spreading the seeds, but it was not ideal for cultivation. In wild grasses, the seeds do not all ripen at the same time, so some of the ears of grain had empty husks by the time the farmers came to harvest them. The farmers reaped only the ears which still contained all the grain, and then sowed only seeds from these grasses. Gradually, wheat with non-scattering seeds evolved.

As farming skills and tools improved,

THE FIRST TOWNS

Groups of farming families built mud-brick houses packed tightly together near their farmland. When the mud bricks eventually crumbled or the houses were destroyed by fire, new houses were built on the ruins of the old ones. A high mound called a 'tell' or a 'hüyük' gradually developed as people continued to build on top of older buildings. When excavated by archaeologists today, they give fascinating clues about how people lived at different times.

Some of these ancient settlements were large enough to be called towns. The first town was probably Jericho, on the River Jordan, but the largest settlement of this period was Catal Hüyük in southern Turkey. Here, craft-workers produced a range of products which could be traded.

Farmers needed pots and baskets for storing food, containers for water and tools for working the land. People needed mats to sleep on and clothes to wear. Ornaments and jewellery made life more attractive. Craft-workers began to work stone, make pots, spin and weave cloth and weave rushes. Some craft-workers started to use a black, volcanic glass-like substance called 'obsidian'. They polished it to make shiny mirrors or shaped it into hard, sharp tools.

Craft-workers needed raw materials for their work. Towns and villages began to trade with each other for these materials and also for the finished crafts and for some foods. Trade links helped people expand their ideas and control and dominate other communities. The great and powerful civilizations that ruled the ancient world all developed from these early farming communities.

CROPS AND ANIMALS

Farmers grew other crops as well as wheat. It was wise to grow several different crops in case one failed. Barley and millet were grown in China. Lentils were a nutritious food grown in some areas such as Syria. Rice was probably first grown in south-east Asia, reaching India and China by about 4000 BC. In Central and South America, farmers grew maize, beans and avocados.

Farmers kept animals for meat, milk and skins. Sheep and goats were among the first animals to be domesticated, though bones at some sites show that farmers sometimes kept gazelles, deer, wild cattle and wild pigs.

TRADING WITHOUT MONEY

Coins were invented in the seventh century BC by the Lydians who lived on the eastern shores of the Mediterranean. Before that time, people had to trade by 'bartering', or exchanging their goods for things of a similar value.

At first, trading was local. Towns had markets where farmers and craft-workers could exchange their goods. As civilizations developed, trade links between different parts of the world were established. In Sumer, for example, there were few raw materials for crafts. The Sumerians had to import what they needed in exchange for the grain they grew on their fertile farmlands.

The earliest traders soon realized that they needed a system of measuring the value of goods. Shells, heads of cattle, gold dust and obsidian were all used as a measure of value for bartering. The Aztecs of Mexico never had money, and continued to barter until their civilization came to an end. The value of something was measured in cloaks or cocoa beans. For example, an Aztec could buy a dug-out canoe for one cloak or one hundred cocoa beans.

GROWING FOOD

By about 5000 BC, agriculture was beginning to spread farther into Europe and Asia. The idea of farming also spread with the movement of people themselves, as some groups searched for new land to cultivate. By 4000 BC, groups of farmers had settled in Italy, Sicily, Malta, northern Africa, Denmark and Sweden. In about 3500 BC, farmers from France crossed to Britain in simple boats.

Not everyone became farmers, though. In North America, for example, there were huge herds of bison which provided enough food and skins for the Native Americans. They had no need to farm. There are still groups of hunter-gatherers today in some parts of the world.

CHOOSING TO FARM

Farmers had to work hard and probably had less leisure time than nomadic people. Even with hard work, a supply of food was not guaranteed. There was always the worry that crops would fail and people would starve. This lifestyle had advantages over the old, nomadic one. Farming gave people the chance to settle down in one place. Hunting became more difficult as the population of the world increased and animals avoided places where people were living. Perhaps some animals were in danger of dying out because so many had been hunted. If this was so, it made sense to grow crops and domesticate animals in an organized way.

A more settled farming lifestyle gave people more control over what they did. They could develop in different ways and form larger and more sophisticated communities. Some people became more powerful than others, and social classes began to develop, with a ruler and rich traders dominating the poorer workers. As trade routes opened up, people became less isolated. They learned what

other communities were doing and could adopt new ideas themselves. Perhaps the idea of farming spread in this way.

We cannot be sure how different communities began to farm because there is not enough evidence. What we do know is that organized production of food was one of the most important discoveries of ancient times and formed the basis of civilization. It is how most of the world's food is produced today.

Watering the crops was a problem for farmers in dry areas, such as the Middle East. They had to invent ways to lift water from a river and carry it to the fields (irrigation). One was the 'shaduf' (above) – a pole with a bucket on one end and a weight on the other. The bucket was lowered into the river and filled with water. The weight on the pole helped to lift the bucket so that it could be emptied into an irrigation ditch.
The man (left) is using a 'shaduf'. The boys (right) are raising water with a treadmill. As they pedal, the paddles go round and scoop up the water.

PLOUGHING THE LAND

When early farmers thought of drawing a branch across the ground to help them turn the soil for sowing, they were on the way to grand-scale agriculture.

The first farmers used very simple tools to prepare the land. Forests often had to be cleared to make a plot of land that could be farmed. The usual method was to burn down the trees. The ash left behind was scattered over the cleared area and the farmer turned the soil with a stick. Sticks were also used to dig holes for planting the seeds. Sometimes, the farmer dug a shallow trench or furrow and sowed a row of seeds. Then, he used a bent stick to cover the seeds with soil.

All this took a long time, so each farmer could only manage to cultivate an area large enough to grow food for himself and his family. As populations grew, this method of farming proved inadequate to feed all the people. Some important developments were needed before food could be produced on a larger scale. One was the invention of the plough. As with many ancient inventions, it is impossible to know who first thought of the idea. Farmers were used to

△ *Oxen are used for pulling ploughs because they are strong and because it is easy to make them move in the right direction.*

28

turning the soil and making short furrows with a digging stick.

Perhaps someone realized that dragging a stick over a longer distance would do the job more quickly, and that a bigger stick would be even more efficient. A bough with forked branches made a simple but effective plough, pulled along by two people. Another person would follow behind, guiding the bough to make sure it was digging into the soil.

THE IDEA SPREADS

No early ploughs have survived, but archaeologists have discovered scratch marks made by ploughs under early settlement mounds. These marks and other evidence such as carvings and wall paintings show us how the plough

spread. The simple scratch plough or 'ard' first appeared in southern Mesopotamia, where plough marks dating back to 4500 BC have been found. Carvings from Uruk and Babylonia also show farmers using scratch ploughs.

From here, the plough seems to have spread to ancient Egypt. Archaeologists excavating an ancient Egyptian tomb dating back to about 2600 BC found a picture of a ploughing scene. By the time of the pharaohs of the Middle Kingdom, from about 2130 to 1777 BC, models and wall paintings of farmers using ploughs were a common sight in tombs.

▽ *Early farmers used a stick with a pointed end to make holes or shallow furrows for sowing seeds. A stone axe might sometimes be needed to break up the hard, dry soil.*

The wooden plough was, by now, an established farming tool in Egypt.

ANIMAL POWER

The earliest scratch ploughs were pulled by people. These ploughs were strong enough to turn the light, dry soils of the Middle East but it was hard work for men to pull a plough for long. It was still only possible to cultivate small areas of land with ploughs pulled in this way.

The domestication of animals developed alongside the cultivation of crops. At first, farmers only thought about meat, milk and skins. Then, they realized that larger animals could be used to do work that was too heavy or difficult for men. One of these tasks was pulling the plough.

Oxen were the first domesticated animals to be used for this purpose. A pair of oxen could pull a plough all day long without getting tired. For the first time, farmers could cultivate large fields and grow enough food to feed a non-farming population as well as themselves.

The use of oxen seems to have been another Mesopotamian development which spread to ancient Egypt. Egyptian tomb paintings and models are our best evidence about what early ploughs looked like. They had a single pole with a pointed end which dug into the ground. This pointed part is known as the 'share'. The plough was steered by a wooden handle fixed to the share. A beam of wood was tied to the top end of the share. Oxen were harnessed to the beam to draw the plough.

PLOUGHS IN EUROPE

Wooden scratch ploughs were suitable for the light soils of Mesopotamia and Egypt, where the weather was dry, but

◁ The first plough was probably a branched bough which was dragged along the ground by two men. A third followed, guiding the bough along the furrow.

△ Oxen were harnessed to the plough by ropes and a wooden beam. They could pull the plough through heavier soils than men could.

they were not so effective on soil that was heavy or wet. Cattle bones found in the lower Danube area of eastern Europe suggest that oxen may have been used to draw ploughs as early as 4500 BC.

There is also evidence that ploughs were being used in Poland and in southern England by about 3500 BC. It would have been hard work to use a wooden plough on the soils of these rainy northern lands, even if it was pulled by animals. Yet that is the only sort of plough there was in the West at this time. The development that was to turn the plough into an efficient tool for large-scale farming on any type of soil came from another region entirely.

CHINESE SECRETS

In China, a civilization was developing quite independently from the other civilizations of the ancient world. Trade and conquest in the West had led to the sharing of knowledge and discoveries throughout Western countries. However, the Chinese guarded their secrets closely and the Orient was to remain a mystery to the West for thousands of years. Yet it was here that some of the most important developments in all sorts of crafts were made. It was Chinese farmers who discovered that stone could be used to make ploughshares much stronger than wooden ones. Stone ploughshares dating back to 3000 BC have been found in China, and they may have been used for far longer. Farmers also used wooden ploughs, but stone, though heavy, could cut deeper furrows through difficult soil.

An even more important Chinese invention was the iron ploughshare. Iron was strong and heavy and it could be shaped into a share that would break up soil very effectively. An iron plough was quicker to use than a wooden or stone one, and it could plough heavy soils more easily. Farmers were using iron ploughs in China by the sixth century BC, at least 500 years before they were discovered by farmers in the West. The Chinese had two types of metal plough. One was made entirely of iron, which would have been effective but heavy. The other type had a wooden share with iron laid over it.

OVERCOMING THE PROBLEMS

In ancient times, iron was usually heated and then beaten into shape to make 'wrought iron'. Another method of shaping iron is to melt it in a furnace, pour it into a mould and let it harden. In this hardened form, it is known as 'cast iron'. Cast iron is a strong, heavy material which could be ideal for making ploughshares. However, it is brittle, so a

THE FIRST PLOUGHS

Though simple, these ploughs enabled the Egyptians and the Mesopotamians to produce large amounts of food to feed their growing populations.

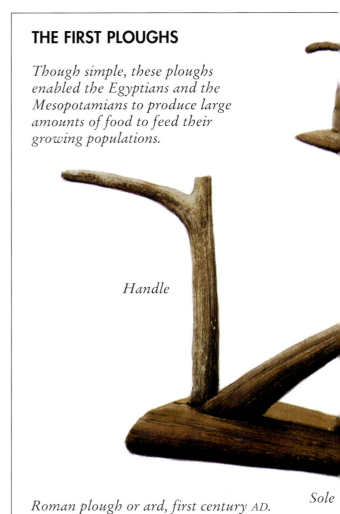

Handle

Roman plough or ard, first century AD.

Sole

PULLING THE PLOUGH

In some parts of the world, farmers still use oxen to pull ploughs over small plots of land. However, this is not such a satisfactory solution for bigger farms because the animals are slow. During the nineteenth century, farmers began to look at other ways of pulling farm machinery.

Steam engines such as the steam tractor were sometimes used for pulling ploughs. However, steam-driven machines were cumbersome and it was difficult to direct the plough over the field properly. The tractors were also heavy and flattened the soil, making it more difficult for the plough to

turn it over. Animals only tread down a small amount of earth and do not affect the work of the plough. A steam plough introduced in 1830 used a system of pulleys and cables to connect a plough to a stationary steam engine. However, many farmers preferred to keep to the traditional methods, and horse-drawn ploughs were still being used in the early part of the twentieth century.

Modern tractors have big wheels which compact the earth to some extent, but they are easier to steer and have the power to pull large, modern ploughs.

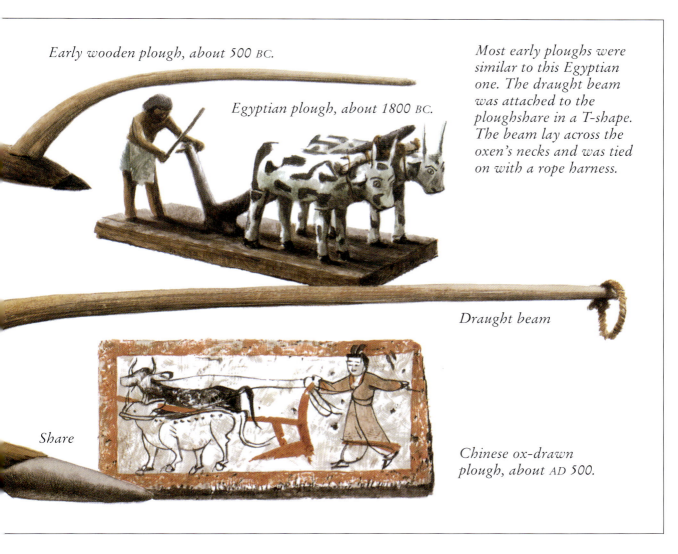

Early wooden plough, about 500 BC.

Egyptian plough, about 1800 BC.

Most early ploughs were similar to this Egyptian one. The draught beam was attached to the ploughshare in a T-shape. The beam lay across the oxen's necks and was tied on with a rope harness.

Draught beam

Share

Chinese ox-drawn plough, about AD 500.

cast iron ploughshare would shatter into fragments if it hit a rock in the soil.

Metal-workers in Europe could not make cast iron at all until the Middle Ages. Intense heat is needed to melt iron and no-one in Europe had found a way of making a powerful enough furnace. Yet the Chinese not only managed to produce cast iron, but they also developed better casting techniques so that they could make cast iron which did not break. This was an amazing achievement.

Firstly, the Chinese found out how to make blast furnaces for melting the iron. By the fourth century BC, they were making furnaces from clay bricks. The clay they used held the heat well, so the

furnaces could reach a high temperature. The Chinese also managed to lower the melting point of iron by mixing it with other minerals. They solved the problem of cast iron's brittleness by keeping the iron at a high temperature for several days, a process known as 'annealing'.

BIGGER AND BETTER
Once the Chinese had worked out how to make stronger iron, they could design bigger and better ploughshares. One problem with early ploughs was that the earth tended to fall back into the furrow as soon as the plough had passed. By the third century BC, Chinese farmers had designed a sharply pointed plough with

wings that flung the earth away to either side of the furrow. These ploughshares could dig deeper furrows than before.

NEAT RIDGES

An even better development for getting rid of the soil from the furrow was the 'mouldboard'. This curved plate above the ploughshare turns the soil over and makes it fall in a neat ridge on one side of the furrow. Chinese farmers were using mouldboards by the first century BC.

Mouldboards did not appear in Europe until medieval times and even then they were not as effective as the Chinese version. The curved mouldboard had a scooping effect which threw the earth well clear of the furrow. European mouldboards were flat, and pushed the earth away from the plough but not far. The ploughman had to keep stopping to clear away soil that had fallen back or stuck to his plough.

◁ A vertical bar called a 'stock' ran from the ploughshare to a handle. The ploughman moved the handle to control the direction of the share in the soil.

Mouldbo

The Chinese also developed another improvement. Soil does not stay the same all the time. It becomes heavy and sticky when it is wet, and light and crumbly when it is dry. There might also be several different soil types within a fairly small area of land.

A farmer had to take these differences into consideration when he ploughed the soil. He had to lean more heavily on the plough handle to push the point of the ploughshare into heavy soil. He had to do the same if he wanted to dig a deeper furrow. The Chinese made a plough that could be adjusted to plough to different depths without the farmer using any extra effort.

EAST MEETS WEST

The Western world did not really know what was going on in China until Europe began to trade with the Chinese. The British and Dutch East India Companies were founded in the early seventeenth century to trade in spices, silks and other products from the East. By the late seventeenth century, the Dutch East India Company had trade routes to China. It was probably these Dutch traders

△ Thomas Jefferson, who helped improve agricultural methods in the USA.

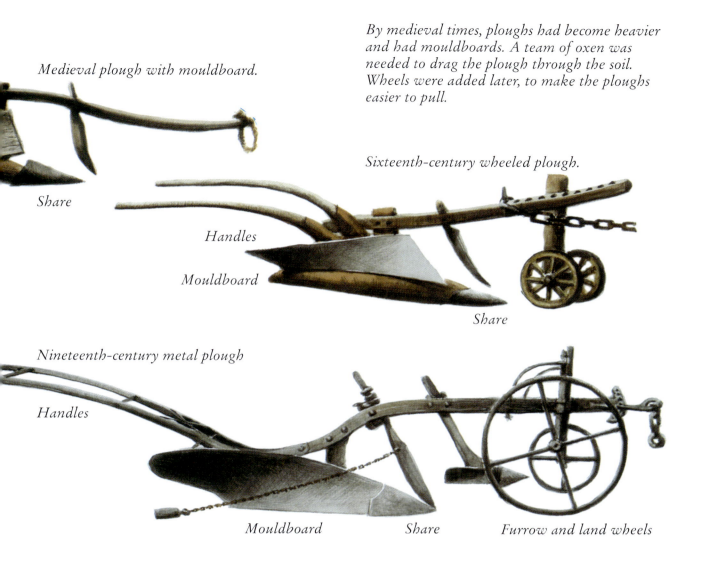

Medieval plough with mouldboard.

By medieval times, ploughs had become heavier and had mouldboards. A team of oxen was needed to drag the plough through the soil. Wheels were added later, to make the ploughs easier to pull.

Share

Sixteenth-century wheeled plough.

Handles

Mouldboard

Share

Nineteenth-century metal plough

Handles

Mouldboard   Share   Furrow and land wheels

brought information about Chinese ploughs to Europe. The Dutch began to use curved mouldboards which they adapted to their own type of soil.

CHANGING THE LANDSCAPE

Farmers in England still used the medieval system of open fields divided into strips. This system was not efficient enough to feed the growing population and, during the eighteenth century, an agricultural revolution swept through the country. Strip farming was replaced by larger fields surrounded by hedges.

The improved plough design was soon adopted by English farmers who needed to plough these larger fields quickly and efficiently. The new style of plough also spread across other parts of northern Europe and to America. Thomas Jefferson (1743-1826), who became President of the United States in 1801, took a great interest in improving methods of agriculture. Some of his ideas came from France, where he had lived in the years leading up to the French Revolution in 1789.

Today's tractor-drawn plough, turning neat furrows in huge modern fields, is a sophisticated machine, but it is still doing the same basic job as the early farmer dragging a stick through the soil.

SCIENTIFIC FARMING

Between 1600 and 1900, the population of the world doubled, and farmers had to face the challenge of feeding and clothing millions more people. To do this, they had to update their working methods, improve their crops and increase their yields.

n 1600, farming all over the world was carried out in much the same way as it had been for thousands of years. The land was divided into small areas, each cultivated by a farmer and his family. In Europe, these areas were often strips just large enough to provide food for the family's own needs. Each farming family also kept a few animals such as sheep or pigs on 'common' land that was set aside for use by everyone.

Life on these small farms was hard. Oxen pulled the ploughs, but almost all the other work was done by the farmer and his family. They sowed seed by 'broadcasting' it, scattering handfuls of seed from a bag as they walked across their fields. When the young plants came up, weeds were kept away by hoeing. Ripe corn and hay were cut with sickles and scythes.

△ *Until the arrival of modern farming methods and machines, even the simplest of jobs, such as hoeing to remove weeds around the crops, were time-consuming manual tasks.*

▷ *In the Middle Ages, fields were divided into strips and each family tended their own crops.*

As long as farms remained small, there was little chance of changing these slow and inefficient methods of farming. Small farmers were content if they managed to feed their families and have a little produce left to sell at the local market. Even if equipment had been available, they did not have any extra money to spend on it. Many even had to borrow or share the oxen they used for ploughing. They could not afford to risk trying out new ideas.

Huge changes in farming began when increasing demand from the growing towns and cities meant a need for more efficient farming methods. Landowners started to take back the land that they had previously leased to the small farmers, and began to cultivate it themselves. The families who had worked the small farms went to work for the landowners, although they were sometimes allowed a little land to grow food for their own tables. The landowners' large farms produced food for the growing non-farming population.

LORD OF THE TURNIPS

One step forward was to introduce changes in the way crops were grown. For many years, farmers had varied the crop on each piece of land from year to year, mainly to prevent plant diseases spreading from one year's crop to the next. From about 1700 onwards, this system of 'rotation' became more scientific, alternating crops such as clover and turnips, which enriched the soil as well as providing animal fodder, with wheat and barley, which were good market crops. Although farmers did not know the scientific reasons why this produced better crops, they found by experience that it did.

The English landowner who became known as the pioneer of this method was Lord Townshend (1674–1738), who owned a large estate in Norfolk. He used a four-year rotation, growing wheat, turnips, barley and clover in his fields in successive years. Townshend was such a keen believer in the benefits of growing turnips on his land that he was given the nickname 'Turnip Townshend'. Like many new farming methods, Townshend's ideas spread slowly, but by the middle of the nineteenth century turnips played their part in the cycle of crops over much of England and increasingly in mainland Europe.

CAST IRON

Meanwhile, another development had sparked off other changes in farming. In 1708, Abraham Darby (1676–1717) opened a foundry in Shropshire in England to make cast iron. Wrought iron had been used to make ploughs in China since about 500 BC, and in Europe about 500 years later, but cast iron was stronger and stayed sharper.

◁ *Lord Townshend was known as 'Turnip Townshend' after the method of crop rotation he advised.*

▷ *Turnips were an ideal fodder crop. Not only could they be eaten by animals and humans, but they also helped to improve the soil for growing other crops.*

The first ploughs using cast iron ploughshares appeared in 1730. These were so expensive that only owners of large farms could afford them.

SPEEDING THE HARVEST

These cast iron tools were simply improvements on earlier versions. The next stage was something completely new. It was to mechanize the most expensive and time-consuming stage in farming: the harvest.

Until the nineteenth century, corn was harvested by hand labour in which everyone in a village, from young children to old people, took part.

The corn was cut by men wielding sickles or scythes. Women and children bound the stalks into sheaves and then stood them in stooks to dry out. Women with rakes gathered up any stalks that the others had missed. The stooks were later collected and taken to a barn.

Once the corn was ripe, the race was on to gather it in and get it under cover. Then came the long task of threshing by hand, using whip-like flails. It took about five days to thresh the corn from half a hectare of land. Finally, the grain was 'winnowed', or tossed in baskets to remove the flakes of chaff, and sorted to separate the larger seeds from the smaller.

▽ *At harvest time, everyone helped out in the fields. Even the very youngest and oldest in the community had their jobs.*

Many people worked on inventions to speed up the harvest. The first target was the long-winded process of threshing.

In 1784, a Scottish inventor called Andrew Meikle (1719–1811) produced a threshing machine with a rotating drum which could be driven by wind, water or horse power. It took less than a day to deal with as much corn as could be threshed by hand in five days. Meikle did not make much money from his invention, and died poor, but his machine, and improved versions of it, greatly speeded up the threshing stage of the harvest. In Britain, it was so successful that farm workers, deprived of their winter work, took to breaking up threshing machines. Later, the machines became even more efficient when they were linked to steam engines.

REAPING MACHINES

Inventors next turned their attention to reaping, or cutting the corn. A gang of five, one cutting the corn with a scythe and the others gathering and binding it, standing it in stooks and raking up the stray stalks, could reap almost a hectare a day. A huge work-force was needed to harvest even a moderately sized farm.

A Scotsman, Patrick Bell (1799–1869), was the inventor of the first efficient

JETHRO TULL AND THE SEED DRILL

Seed drills to replace the inefficient method of sowing seeds by broadcasting were used in Mesopotamia over 5,000 years ago, but in most farms in the Western world, seed continued to be broadcast until well into the nineteenth century.

The first successful seed drill in the West was invented by an English lawyer turned farmer, Jethro Tull (1674–1741). He made his first horse-drawn drill, using a spring-loaded flap to control the flow of seed to the soil, in 1701. Tull was a musician, and he took the idea of the spring-loaded flap from the mechanism of a church organ. Tull's drill not only spread the seed more evenly, but the fact that it sowed in rows meant that hoeing and harvesting became easier. However, most farmers preferred to rely on the old method, and it was not until about 150 years later that drilling became the normal method of sowing.

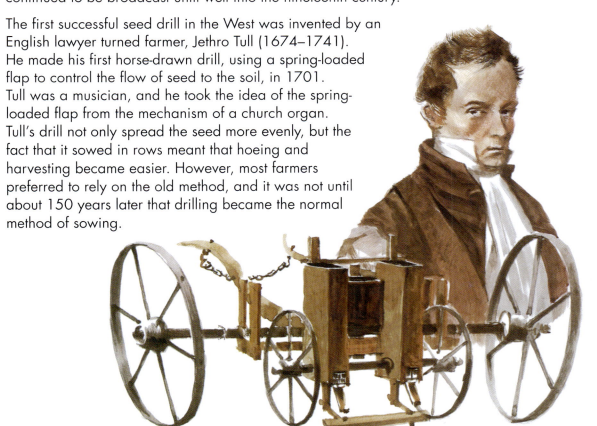

SCIENTIFIC FARMING

▷ *Most of the machines invented during the mid-nineteenth century to speed up the harvest were unsuccessful.*

△ *In Bell's Reaper, produced in 1826, the mechanism was pushed in front of the horses.*

▷ *It was not until McCormick's reaper, produced in the 1840s, that the mechanization of the harvest finally took off.*

△ *Obed Hussey (1792–1860) produced his machine in 1837. In his reaper, the cutting mechanism was at the side of the machine.*

reaper. He demonstrated it in 1826 and it won a prize, but few farmers were interested. Other inventors had the same experience. It was not until the 1840s, when an American, Cyrus McCormick (1809–84), began to sell the reaper that he had invented, that the idea of mechanized harvesting took off.

FARMING THE PRAIRIES

McCormick chose just the right moment to launch his machine. The American West was just opening up, and pioneer farmers

saw the possibilities of growing vast quantities of wheat on the prairies, if only they could harvest it quickly. But there were simply not enough people on the isolated prairie homesteads to harvest by hand. McCormick made it easy for American farmers to buy his machine by letting them pay for it over 18 months. That way, they could buy it out of the profits of a year's harvest. The other important feature of the McCormick reaper was that it was mass-produced, using identical parts. If a part failed, it could be easily replaced. Having sold well in North America, the McCormick reaper arrived in Europe. Soon, McCormick's factory was turning out 4,000 reapers a year.

Once reaping and threshing machines had both been invented, the next stage was to combine the two operations in one machine. That way, a machine could move into a field of standing corn and leave it with the corn already cut, threshed, bagged and ready for market. The first horse-drawn machine of this kind appeared in the USA in the 1830s, although it was not widely used until the 1870s. It was called the 'combination harvester', and was the ancestor of today's combine harvester.

PLOUGHING BY STEAM

Meanwhile, attempts were made to find a cheaper alternative to horses as a source of power on the farm. Horses had to be bred and trained for their work. They needed feeding, care and skilled control. After the invention of the steam engine in the late eighteenth century, efforts were made to use steam as a source of power for farming. Steam power could be used with Andrew Meikle's threshing machine and its successors, and threshing gangs moved from farm to farm with their machines, following the harvest. Steam power was also used for ploughing, with one or two engines pulling a plough on a cable from one side of a field to the other. However, only the largest and most adventurous farmers used steam to plough. True mechanization of farming had to await the invention of the petrol-driven tractor, and, later, the diesel versions, in the early 1900s. Even then, because of the cost of tractors and fuel, many small farmers went on using horses for ploughing until the 1940s and 1950s.

BREEDING THE BEST

Arable farming, or the production of crops from the soil, is only one side of agriculture. The other is the raising of livestock for milk, wool and meat. Livestock farming also made a scientific leap forward from the eighteenth century.

For centuries, farmers had bred from their best animals to produce livestock that gave more meat or wool, or that were more suited to their environment. The growing of the new fodder crops

△ *Bakewell's Leicestershire sheep.*

△ *During the late nineteenth century, teams of workers would travel around the country with steam threshers, stopping to work wherever they were needed.*

such as clover and turnips led to an improvement in livestock generally, and inspired many farmers to experiment with selective breeding to improve their stock still more.

One of the great pioneers of selective breeding was a Leicestershire man, Robert Bakewell (1725–95). He was about 20 when he began his experiments in sheep breeding. The result was the Leicestershire breed of sheep. They were small-boned, barrel-shaped animals with short legs and small heads. Leicestershires fattened quickly, producing saleable meat in two years instead of the usual four. Bakewell also emphasized the importance of good fodder, shelter and handling.

SPREADING THE WORD

Leicestershire sheep were more expensive than other breeds, and Bakewell's recommendations on animal care meant that his methods could be followed only on the more prosperous farms.

These included the farms on the estates of Thomas Coke (1752–1842, pronounced 'Cook') in Norfolk and the fifth Duke of Bedford (1765–1802) in the English Midlands. Both of these immensely rich landowners played a part in spreading the new scientific farming ideas. Both held annual 'Sheep Shearings' which were Britain's first agricultural shows, and built model farms where up-to-date methods of livestock and arable farming were demonstrated to interested visitors.

FIND OUT SOME MORE

After you have read about the ideas and inventions in this book, you may want to find out some more information about them. There are lots of books devoted to specific topics, such as farming or early people, so that you can discover more facts. All over Britain and Ireland, you can see historical sites and visit museums that contain historical artefacts that will tell you more about the subjects that interest you. The books, sites and museums listed below cover some of the most important topics in this book. They are just a start!

GENERAL INFORMATION
BOOKS
These books all present a large number of inventions of all different kinds:

Oxford Illustrated Encyclopedia of Invention and Technology edited by Sir Monty Finniston (Oxford University Press, 1992)

Usborne Illustrated Handbook of Invention and Discovery by Struan Reid (Usborne, 1986)

Invention by Lionel Bender (Dorling Kindersley, 1986)

The Way Things Work by David Macaulay (Dorling Kindersley, 1988)

Key Moments in Science and Technology by Keith Wicks (Hamlyn, 1999)

A History of Invention by Trevor I. Williams (Little Brown, 1999)

WEBSITE
For information on many different inventions, visit: http://inventors.about.com

MUSEUMS
Many large museums contain interesting artefacts related to people of the past, and some have collections that may be more specifically about some of the themes covered in this book.

To find out more about the museums in your area, ask in your local library or tourist information office, or look in the telephone directory.

A useful guide is *Museums & Galleries in Great Britain & Ireland* (British Leisure Publications, East Grinstead) which tells you about over 1,300 places to visit. For a good introduction to the subjects covered in this book, visit:

Science Museum, Exhibition Road, London SW7 www.sciencemuseum.org.uk

For displays and information about many of the earliest ideas and inventions, go to:

British Museum, Great Russell Street, London WC1 www.britishmuseum.co.uk

WEBSITES
For general information about the history of farming, visit;
www.historylink101.com/lessons/farm-city/story-of-farming.htm

PREHISTORIC PEOPLE
BOOKS
Prehistoric People by Tim Wood (Franklin Watts, 1980)

MUSEUMS
Almost all large, general museums have some information and artefacts related to prehistoric people. These may just be a few flints, or a much larger collection. Check with your local museum.

SITES
Iceni Village and Museums, Cockley Cley, Swaffham Norfolk
www.information-britain.co.uk
An Iron Age, Celtic village, where they stage 'reconstruction days'.

The ARC, St Saviourgate, York
www.jorvik-viking-centre.co.uk/arc
A 'hands-on' archaeology exhibition, where visitors can sift through ancient remains to find out about people of the past.

Lough Gur Stone Age Centre, Bruff Road, Holycross, Co. Limerick, Eire
One of Ireland's most important archaeological sites.

Jarlshof Prehistoric Site, Sumburgh, Shetland

Skara Brae, Dounby, Orkney
www.orkneyjar.com/history/skarabrae
A complex of houses over 4,000 years old.

EARLY FARMING
MUSEUMS
Many country areas have farming museums where you can see old farming tools and methods, and often look at unusual old breeds of animals, too. Ask at the local library or tourist centre.

Butser Ancient Farm, Gravel Hill, Horndean, Hants
www.butser.org.uk
This reconstructed Iron Age farm (c. 1500 BC onwards) is farmed using Iron Age and Roman techniques. There is an education centre where you can find out what it was like to be a prehistoric farmer.

FARMING
BOOKS
Investigating the Story of Farm Animals by Gillian Osband (National Trust, 1991)

INDEX